## Hello?
### Compton, 1957

A working mobile telephone painted metallic
copper to match the car's exterior is the perfect
finishing touch to Donna Alcorn's customized 1957 Ford.

Vista Dunes Trailer Park

Indio, 1958

Charles Phoenix

# Southern Californialand

## Mid-Century Culture in Kodachrome®

ACP
Angel City Press

Design by Amy Inouye

# Images

# Winter in
# Southern California
## Pasadena and Palm Springs, 1956

A luxurious and powerful 1955 Cadillac Eldorado Biarritz convertible pulls over near the corner of Walnut Street and Allen Avenue in Pasadena. One of just 3,950 produced, it's the most extreme and ostentatious car on the road. It complements this picture-perfect postcard view of winter in Southern California—the crystal-clear blue sky, palm trees blowing in the breeze, fragrant orange groves and snow-capped Mt. Baldy are a dramatic backdrop. The owner of the Cadillac is Mary Marr, in her swimsuit on the opposite page. She strikes a pose inside her bungalow at the Desert Inn, a world-famous winter resort in Palm Springs, where she is the hostess. She is living the glamorous life.

## Snow Day!
### Uptown Whittier, 1949

January 11—From Santa Monica to San Diego, a freak snowstorm blankets
Southern California. It is the first time the Los Angeles Unified School
District declares a "snow day" and closes the schools.

# Shriners' Arabian Bazaar
## Pershing Square, Downtown Los Angeles, 1950

Welcome, Nobles. Taken from the Biltmore Hotel, this view of the festivities
in Pershing Square captures not only the Shriners in their fezzes, but the
fez painted on the door of the 1950 Ford Custom Convertible Coupe.

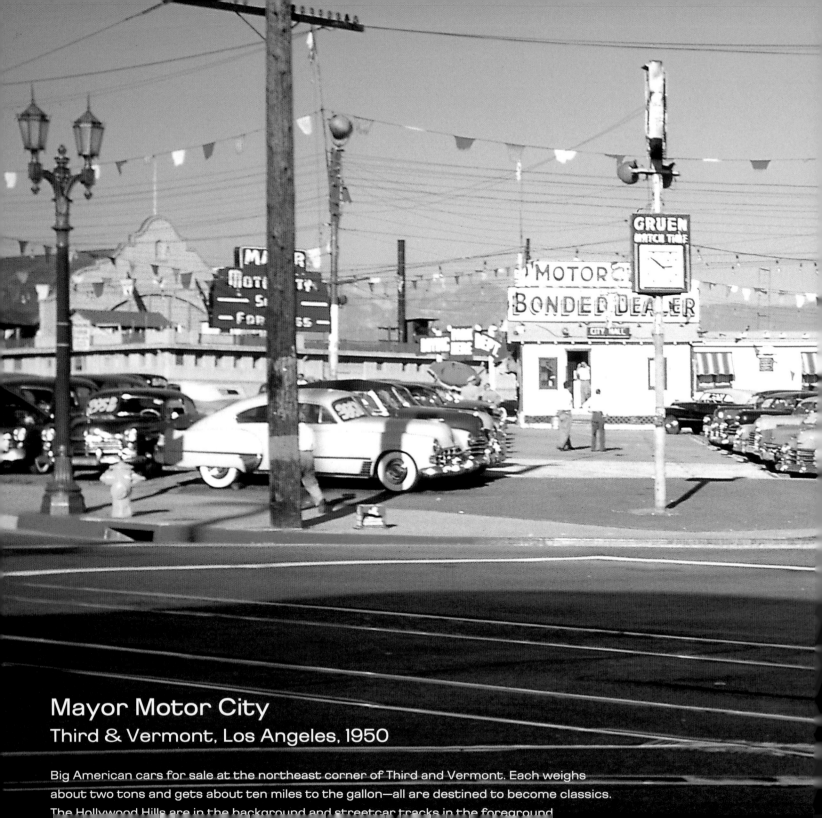

# Mayor Motor City
## Third & Vermont, Los Angeles, 1950

Big American cars for sale at the northeast corner of Third and Vermont. Each weighs about two tons and gets about ten miles to the gallon—all are destined to become classics. The Hollywood Hills are in the background and streetcar tracks in the foreground.

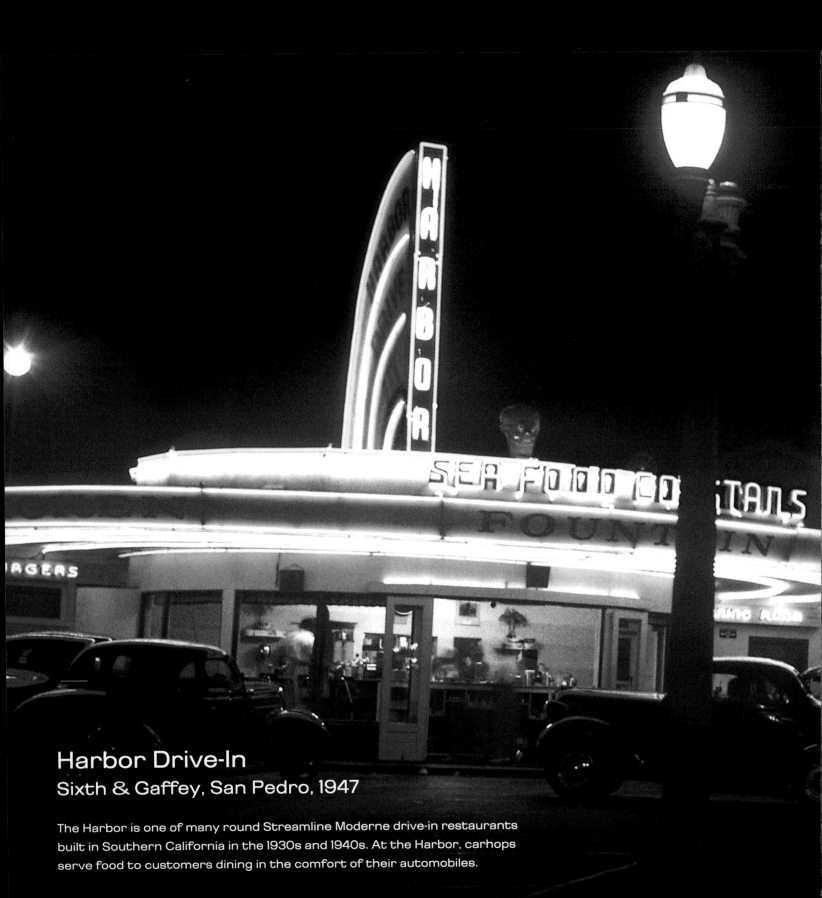

# Harbor Drive-In
## Sixth & Gaffey, San Pedro, 1947

The Harbor is one of many round Streamline Moderne drive-in restaurants built in Southern California in the 1930s and 1940s. At the Harbor, carhops serve food to customers dining in the comfort of their automobiles.

Entertainment
CHICKEN   STEAK   SQUAB

DANCING          COCKTAILS

ASSOCIATED

RICHFIELD

## Chinatown
### Downtown Los Angeles, 1955

This in-camera, multi-exposure image captures the variety of neons that make Chinatown glow by night. The City of Los Angeles created this themed environment in 1939.

# Olvera Street
## Downtown Los Angeles, 1960

Once the heart and soul of Los Angeles, in 1930 Olvera Street became the city's first urban renewal project, turning a slum into a must-see tourist attraction.

# Children's Hospital Auxiliary Luncheon
## Palos Verdes, 1953

Models pose at the edge of a cliff in front of a windbreak at a high-class
Pacific Ocean-side/poolside fashion show.

Entrance to Tomorrowland
Disneyland, Anaheim, 1960

Walt Disney's original Tomorrowland is promoted as "The World of 1987."

# Introduction

Other peoples' old family and travel slides from the 1940s, '50s and '60s were the last thing I was looking for when I first stepped into a thrift store in my hometown of Ontario, California. It was 1977. I was fourteen years old and looking for a cowboy shirt to wear in a local production of *Oklahoma!* Not only did I find the perfect cowboy shirt, I found a whole new wardrobe, and my never-ending secondhand shopping spree began. It didn't take long for me to realize that thrift shops were the seductive underbelly of our mass consumer culture. Through my teens and twenties I considered thrift shops to be museums of merchandise and schools of style. I made the rounds as often as possible.

Fast forward to when I was thirty and had just begun to question my secondhand shopaholic ways. In a little thrift shop in Pasadena, I discovered a most unexpected treasure, a treasure that would change the course of my life. It was an old blue shoebox marked "Trip across the United States, 1957." Inside were dozens of 35mm Kodachrome slides of some anonymous family's vacation. I held a few up to the light and knew that I'd found a time machine in a box.

The idea of time traveling with people I didn't know and enjoying their vacation right along with them—thirty-five years later—was very intriguing to me. Immediately I knew it was my mission in life to rescue as many orphaned slide collections as possible. I began going to thrift shops, flea markets and estate sales looking for one thing and one thing only—old slides. Rarely did I come home without a box or bag full. I would go through each newfound collection like it was an unwritten book and my job was to find its story. By looking at every detail and reading

## Say Cheese!
Los Angeles, 1956

what, if anything, had been handwritten on the card-board mounts, I began to piece together the stories of each family's life. The pastime became an obsession, a fascinating addiction.

As the histories took shape, I began sharing my favorite images with friends by having slide shows in my living room. One night a friend suggested that I do a slide show at the California Map and Travel Center in Santa Monica. The idea of sharing my favorites with a broader audience inspired me. But when I spoke to the owners of the store about showing old vacation slides, they looked at me as if I was completely nuts. They assured me that nobody would ever be interested in looking at other peoples' old slides. But I knew better. I went back a few days later with a few of my best selections in hand and got the gig. That was in 1998. I've been doing vintage slide show presentations ever since.

I'm still collecting slides, but now they come to me. People give me their family slides. Sometimes they even leave them on my doorstep. One evening after a performance, a man came up to me and said "I've got all my dad's old slides and I want you to have them. My dad always dreamed of being a photojournalist but never was." His father may not have thought he achieved his dream, but to me he did. Four of his amazing shots are in this book; the Harbor Drive-In and the Ice Cream Pony Cart in San Pedro, the Shriners' Arabian Bazaar in Pershing Square, and Seventh & Broadway in downtown Los Angeles. Another after-a-slide-show donation became the cover of this book. I couldn't believe it when I first saw it—a perfect Southern California shot. One day I walked into an estate sale and bought a box of slides marked "10 Com." When I got home and opened it, I found three hundred fifty Kodachrome slides taken behind the scenes on the set of the 1956 Academy Award-winning film *The Ten Commandments*. That was a great day.

Occasionally I'll be invited to borrow slides from a personal collection. Such is the case with the slide of McDonald's on page 81. This very rare color shot from the early days of fast food is one of only two shots of the stylish hamburger stand taken by Charles Fish, who engineered the legendary Golden Arches. He was the assistant to the architect. Those are the only shots of an early McDonald's that I've ever seen in color.

Most amateur slide collections average one or two of what I call "showable" slides. At worst, a collection is a bunch of underexposed, out-of-focus pictures of barren scenery. At best, there's a box with two or three real gems. But after editing and cataloguing so many thousands of slides, I realize that what may have seemed like just a sentimental "Kodak moment" at the time is history now. These images are treasures.

Southern California and Kodachrome slide photography came of age at the same time. After World War II, Kodak began promoting 35mm Kodachrome slide film (which had been introduced to professionals in 1936) to amateur photographers just as Southern California was becoming America's suburban frontier. Master-planned communities, fantasy theme parks and the spirited car culture that defined the region also defined the American dream. Richness of color, depth of light and shadow, and resistance to fading made Kodachrome the greatest mass-marketed film ever invented and a miracle—in a way—of modern science.

# Pacific Ocean Park Entrance
## Santa Monica, 1958

Spinning, translucent seahorses are the perfect topping to this giant space-age starfish. Though similar in design, the entrance to Pacific Ocean Park predates the Theme Building that opens in 1961 at Los Angeles International Airport. Ocean Park Amusement Pier, which dates back to the turn of the century, got a total makeover and became Pacific Ocean Park, a theme park with an oceanic motif. It fails after nine years and closes in 1967.

While the local postwar economy boomed and Southern California became a cultural and creative superpower, a generation of mom-and-pop photographers embraced the luxurious new photo medium. For the first time amateurs were able to personally and spontaneously document their everyday lives and the rapidly changing region around them in living color that rivaled the Technicolor they saw at the movie theater (Kodachrome had originally been introduced in 1935 as 16mm motion picture film). Ironically, during that same era, the vast majority of professional photographers captured their subjects in black and white. So it was really the moms and pops who provided us with the best photographic record of Southern California's colorful mid-century cultural explosion. Today digital technology has made 35mm slide photographs relics of the past. The heyday of Kodachrome film is long over. In fact, by 2005 Kodak will no longer manufacture the film Paul Simon penned a song about.

By now I've looked at millions of old slides and the subjects of my collection span the globe. But I most cherish the slides taken in Southern California. Growing up in Southern California in the 1960s and '70s, and never having lived anywhere else, I have a personal connection to many of the images I've been lucky enough to find and include in this book. Some of my earliest childhood memories are of the Saturday mornings that I spent at my dad's used car lots getting in and out of each automobile—pretending to drive every one. They are the same models that show up in these slides. I remember sitting on the fold-down armrest in the backseat of my grandparents' pink '58 Cadillac Sedan de Ville on the way to Eastland Shopping Center in West Covina. Our first stop was always the May Co. Then we would have lunch there at Clifton's Cafeteria, which unlike the original downtown, was ultramodern. When I was nine I met the Brady Bunch. They were promoting

# Family Portrait
## Huntington Beach, 1955

Disneyland
PARK & HOTEL · ENTRANCE
OPEN EVERYDAY
TODAY 9-12
HOTEL & RESTAURANT OPEN

their Christmas album at White Front, a discount department store in Ontario. And of course we went to all the theme parks. I was awed by porpoises jumping through flaming hoops at Marineland in Palos Verdes, and nourished by Mrs. Knott's famous fried chicken dinner at Knott's Berry Farm.

But the most eagerly anticipated and fondly remembered days of my childhood were when we went to Disneyland. In 1969, when I was six, I watched man's first steps on the moon live on a big-screen monitor in Tomorrowland. Then I rode the Flight to the Moon afterwards. That made a big impression on me. My family went to Disneyland three or four times every year. Looking back, now it seems like it was part of my education. My childhood memories of the park still inspire my imagination today—I see a bit of Disneyland all over Southern California. I can picture Los Angeles International Airport's space-age Theme Building in Tomorrowland, or the exotica of Old Chinatown and Olvera Street in Adventureland. It's easy for me to imagine Knott's Berry Farm's ghost town as part of Frontierland, or the Big Do-Nut Drive-In right next to the giant teacups in Fantasyland and Angel's Flight on Main Street USA. In many ways the Magic Kingdom defines the eclectic personality of Southern California.

Southern California's collective history is all here in rich, clear Kodachrome, thanks to the families who unwittingly documented an era and then cast away the records of the times of their lives. As fate has delivered their slides to me, it's my privilege to share some of my very favorites with you. So sit back, relax and enjoy this retro slide show tour of the people and places, scenes and situations of America's new world—a very magical kingdom I lovingly call Southern Californialand.

—Charles Phoenix, 2004

# Original Disneyland Sign
## Anaheim, 1960

# Theme Building
## Los Angeles International Airport, 1967

An observation deck, restaurant and cocktail lounge combo in the middle of a parking lot—they comprise the most spectacular space-age structure on earth. This timeless marvel of engineering and design is the centerpiece of the 1961 jet-age expansion of Los Angeles International Airport.

Complemented by a never-ending parade of jet planes taking off and landing and Sputnik-light fixtures in the parking lot, the Theme building is like nothing else in this world. Its entrance is politely secluded behind a circular wall of perforated cement blocks. Travelers enter through the Court of Stars Lobby, which is decorated with enormous backlit transparencies of faraway galaxies. Seventy feet above, guests dine in the circular, split-level "sky high" restaurant while taking in the breathtaking bird's-eye view of the new airport. For those who want the ultimate view, there's a rooftop observation deck. The Theme Building is the collaborative work of four of Southern California's greatest architects: Charles Luckman, William Pereira, Welton Becket and Paul Williams. According to legend, it is designed to resemble a spaceship, inspired by the movie *War of the Worlds* (Paramount, 1954), whose art director is Pereira's brother, Hal. The futuristic design is an obvious inspiration for the fantasy architecture of *The Jetsons* which made its debut in 1962, a year after the Theme Building was dedicated.

In the parking lot a 1965 Rambler Marlin, the sportiest model in the American Motors line-up, has a fastback roofline, floor shift console and bucket seats.

# Marineland of the Pacific
## Palos Verdes, 1957

A spectacular setting with a picture-perfect view. Ninety acres on a choice bluff high above the crashing waves of the Pacific Ocean. On a clear day you can see Catalina Island. There is no site more ideal for "The World's Largest Oceanarium." Opened in 1954, Marineland is home to a wide variety of more than four thousand sea creatures including whales, walruses, sea lions, porpoises and penguins. The ultramodern aquarium/stadium structure should be dubbed "The Aquadium." George Foster, founder of Foster Freeze, a local soft-serve franchise, operates the Marineland restaurant and Porpoise Room cocktail lounge. Building contractors and structural engineers call Marineland a monumental feat of engineering and claim it is earthquake-proof. God forbid the whole thing should crack open during a temblor and all those fish wash right down the cliff into the ocean where they came from!

During its heyday, Marineland is considered a must-see tourist attraction. In 1987, the corporation that owns Sea World in San Diego buys Marineland vowing to keep the park operating, but closes it one month later.

# North Shore Beach and Yacht Club
## Salton Sea, 1958

This is ultra-modern desert style on a budget. Porthole windows are shaded with bias-cut cylinders, corrugated aluminum, yellow fiberglass and sandy pink cinderblocks. It is the imaginative work of legendary architect Albert Frey of Palm Springs. The nautical theme clubhouse/coffee shop/cocktail lounge is built in the shape of a ship's bridge. The American flag blows in the desert breeze from a mast-like flagpole. The sea-worthy flag designs across the front hang like modern art. Palm trees provide ambience; umbrellas provide shade.

      The Salton Sea is just that, a salty body of water that's twenty-five percent saltier than the ocean. It was formed unexpectedly when a Colorado River levee burst in 1905 and flowed for two years into an ancient dry lake bed in the middle of the desert. Right after World War II, real estate and resort developers had big plans for the Salton Sea. They began promoting it as America's Riviera, a "new year-round water sports playground." Utopian master-planned communities complete with marinas, motels, shopping centers and golf courses were planned, but most were never built. Miraculously, this futuristic Yacht Club will still be standing beyond the year 2000, but in ruin.

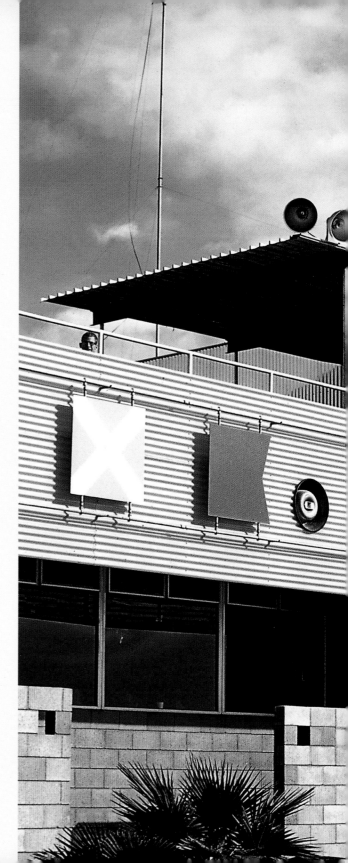

# House of the Future
## Disneyland, Anaheim, 1966

Between 1957 and 1967, this three-bedroom, two-bath, model dream house stands at the end of Main Street USA between Sleeping Beauty's Castle and the entrance to Tomorrowland. Monsanto sponsors the popular walk-through exhibit. The brochure boasts "not a natural material in the house;" the dynamic structure is made entirely of plastic. Microwave cooking, electric toothbrushes, big-screen television, molded furniture and push-button telephones are seen here for the first time by most visitors. The House of the Future is a startling contrast to the countless ranch-style tract homes that are being built in the rest of Southern California. A cross between a giant marshmallow and an enormous wheel of cheese, it looks more like a work of modern art than a house. Its cantilevered wings float above the surface, making the structure suitable for any terrain. Beneath the wings is space for two shaded carports, a patio and play area. Inside the pedestal foundation, from which the house blossoms, is the climate-control center, which heats the house, cools it, purifies its air and scents the interior with the fragrance of pine trees, sea air or freshly cut flowers. In 1967, Tomorrowland gets a complete makeover and the "old" House of the Future is out of date and has to go. But the structure proves to be very sturdy and the wrecking ball bounces right off the plastic walls, forcing the demolition crew to destroy it by hand.

# Wagon Camp
## Knott's Berry Farm, Buena Park, 1957

Children square dance, do-si-doin' their partners to toe-tappin' and knee-slappin' music performed by "America's Youngest Western Band, the Cactus Kids" at the main entertainment stage in Ghost Town. The best seats in the house—authentic covered wagons from pioneer days—surround the horseshoe-shaped amphitheater. At night, around the campfire, folks gather to hear pioneer stories and sing songs of the Old West.

In 1920, Walter and Cordelia Knott began farming berries and selling them roadside in the rural town of Buena Park. By 1927, Mrs. Knott had opened a little dining room next to the fruit stand where she served hot biscuits and berry jam, berry pie and coffee. While experimenting with new berry varieties in 1932, Mr. Knott discovered a cross between a raspberry, blackberry and loganberry. He named it the boysenberry in honor of the neighboring farmer who propagated it, Rudolph Boysen. Those boysens were big, sweet and juicy berries, easy to grow and even easier to sell. The enterprising farmers were in for even more success when Mrs. Knott added fried chicken dinners to her menu in 1934. They expanded the dining room but never could accommodate the weekend crowds. To entertain people while they waited, Mr. Knott began building a ghost town in 1940.

Knott's Berry Farm evolves into a total-immersion environment where architecture, costumed employees, performances, merchandise, music and transportation are based on an authentic 1880s Gold Rush boom town. It is homespun, family run and, more importantly, it's America's first "theme park."

# Dinosaur
## Cabazon, 1970

The desert's most famous drive-by landmark, the giant freeway-side brontosaurus is the creation of Claude Bell, a man who has spent many years working for Knott's Berry Farm and Warner Bros. motion picture studio building miniatures and models.

Dinosaur construction began in 1964 when Mr. Bell was seventy-three. For the next few years, speeding motorists watch from the freeway as the dinosaur takes shape, gets covered with a cement skin and painted to look like the real thing. By the time Mr. Bell is finished in 1974, the man who spent his career making miniatures has created the largest dinosaur in the United States. "Dinny" as Mr. Bell referred to him, is one hundred fifty feet long, three times life-size. Inside the tummy of the Jurassic giant, Mr. Bell opens a gift shop accessible from a rear-entry staircase. After building a second giant dinosaur on the site, a fifty-five-foot-tall Tyrannosaurus Rex, Claude Bell dies in 1989. His dinosaurs become two of Southern California's most famous roadside icons.

# The Towers of Simon Rodia— Watts Towers
## Los Angeles, 1960

Soaring majestically above the community for which they are named, Watts Towers transform a simple working-class neighborhood in South Central Los Angeles into a world-class destination for folk art lovers. One man, Simon Rodia, created the Watts Towers by hand in the triangle-shaped side yard of his home. Over the course of thirty-three years, between 1921 and 1954, he shaped the towers with scrap steel pipes, then covered them with bottle caps, seashells and colorful broken bits and pieces of glass and pottery. In 1959, the city declared the Towers to be unsafe, and demolition seemed inevitable. But folk art fans from around the world protested and prevailed. Tests and time prove the durability of Rodia's whimsical structures. To walk among them is magical.

# Oil Derricks
## Signal Hill, 1953

One of Southern California's chief exports over the last hundred years, besides movies, is oil. Between the turn of the century and the late 1950s, the old-style wooden oil derricks were a common sight in the oil-rich cities of Los Angeles, Torrance, Wilmington, La Habra, Huntington Beach and Sante Fe Springs.

Per acre, Signal Hill is one of the most productive fields the world has ever known.

The wooden oil structures are extremely flammable, so by the mid 1960s many of them are replaced with the new metal "bobbing mule" style derricks.

# Pacific Electric Red Cars • Bellflower, 1958

May 25—thick black smoke fills the sky. The Hancock Oil Refinery in Long Beach is burning. It's the day of the last run of the Red Car line that has carried passengers between downtown Los Angeles and Bellflower for more than fifty years. Jim Walker of Lynwood, a lifelong Red Car enthusiast, is there to take slides. He couldn't have asked for a more dramatic backdrop. That's him posing. The Pacific Electric Red Car system began in

1901. By 1920 there were more than nine hundred cars connecting five counties and it was one of, if not *the* world's largest inter-urban trolley systems. After World War II, officials claimed the system was antiquated and had to go. Line by line, the vast network is dismantled. The last Red Car runs in 1961. All but two of the cars are scrapped: one goes to the Trolley Museum in Perris and the other to Travel Town in Griffith Park.

# Broadway & Seventh
## Downtown Los Angeles, 1947

The busiest intersection in town is bustling with activity. An electric "streamliner" streetcar heads north on Broadway. A banner blows in the morning breeze. Broadway is one of the few streets in Los Angeles that actually looks like a traditional American big city. Lined with more department stores, specialty shops, cafeterias and movie theaters than anywhere else in Southern California, it is the retail and entertainment hub of the city. For more than fifty years, beginning just after the turn of the century, Broadway, between Fourth and Ninth Streets, has been a destination location for the masses who come from the suburbs, primarily by streetcar. On the west side of the street stands Bullock's department store, Le Roys jewelry store, Kress five-and-dime, and the baroque fantasy-inspired Los Angeles Theatre. Across the street are Clifton's Brookdale Cafeteria, the clothing stores Harris & Frank and Bond, and the Palace Theatre. During the 1950s, Broadway begins to evolve into a multi-cultural marketplace. The KRKD radio tower continues to broadcast until 1961. In 1963, the last streetcar runs in downtown Los Angeles. In the 1980s preservationists recognize Broadway as having the largest concentration of historic movie palaces in the world.

# Angel's Flight • Downtown Los Angeles, 1956

From 1901 to 1969, the most charming transportation system in town, a steep funicular railroad designed by J.W. Eddy, carries passengers up and down Bunker Hill at the corner of Third and Hill Streets. During that time, the hilltop evolves from a fashionable neighborhood of Victorian homes and apartments to a slum. In 1959 Angel's Flight is slated for demolition as part of the Bunker Hill Urban Renewal Project. Rail enthusiasts fight to preserve it as a landmark and are successful until 1969, when the city dismantles the funicular, promising to rebuild it in two years. Twenty-seven years later, in 1996, Angel's Flight is reconstructed a half-block from its original site. Tragically, in 2001, the cable snaps, the cars crash, a passenger is killed, and Angel's Flight is closed.

# Bunker Hill to Hollywood
## West from the top of City Hall, 1957

Southern California's famous four-level freeway interchange is on the right, and the Hollywood sign is visible in the hills. The building under construction on the left is the Los Angeles County courthouse.

# Los Angeles City Hall
## Downtown Los Angeles, 1955

Reflected in the window of the Superior Court Assembly Room are the County Hall of Records and Los Angeles City Hall. The photographer titles this slide, "Waiting."

By law, Los Angeles City Hall is the tallest building in town until the city council abandons height restrictions in 1957 and Union Bank building—the city's first sky-scraper—is completed in 1966. City Hall's supreme height always has given it star quality—it was cast in the original 1950s *Superman* television series as home to the *Daily Planet* and is the featured building on the original *Dragnet*. Like the eclectic city it stands for, style-wise it is a mish-mash of old world and Art Deco architecture and appoint-ments, both inside and out. The unique and instantly-recognizable crowning touch, the stair-stepped pyramid, was inspired by one of the seven wonders of the ancient world, the Mausoleum at Halicarnassus. The Dedication Day press releases from 1928 claimed that among its construction materials was sand from each of California's fifty-eight counties and cement from each of the state's cement mills mixed with water from each of its twenty-one missions.

# Bunker Hill
## Downtown Los Angeles, 1963

The new Bunker Hill, Los Angeles by night. Traffic is streaming by and the Department of Water and Power, Bunker Hill's first ultramodern building, is all aglow. Modern downtown Los Angeles has begun to take shape. The Long Beach Camera Club has gathered downtown to capture the city on film. A man and his wife, both members of the club, are photographed by another member as their 1959 Triumph breaks down at the southwest corner of Grand and First. Her oil painting immortalizes an overgrown and abandoned Victorian house as her husband looks under the hood.

Months later, the camera club costume party convenes in the Long Beach living room of the man who took these slides. The painter is the baseball player, the mechanic is the monkey and our photographer is in red overalls with a rubber snake on his head.

# The Last Mansion and the First Skyscraper
## Bunker Hill, Downtown Los Angeles, 1969

The Donegan Castle was built circa 1882 and the Union Bank building was dedicated in 1966.

By 1969, after a decade of demolition, there was almost nothing from the turn of the twentieth century left standing on Bunker Hill. As Southern California prospers, the fashionable late-nineteenth century hilltop neighborhood of Victorians, that has become a slum, has all but disappeared from the cityscape. While the Department of Water and Power building, Music Center and Union Bank give the city a new modern skyline, the D.F. Donegan House remains as a monument to the old Bunker Hill and the early days of Los Angeles.

In 1964, preservationists won their battle to save the mansion called "The Castle." It is declared Historic-Cultural Monument No. 27, and is destined to be moved to a new site, Heritage Square in Highland Park. The night before the long-awaited move, shortly after this photo is taken, vandals torch the landmark mansion and it burns to the ground.

## Queen Mary
### Long Beach Harbor, 1967

December 9—just after nine in the morning and the waters are choppy. The harbor is crowded with boats full of spectators here to see the *RMS Queen Mary* at the end of her final voyage. After one thousand and one crossings of the Atlantic Ocean, just thirty-one years after her maiden voyage in 1936, she is suddenly an obsolete relic. The *Queen Mary* is one of the grandest ocean liners ever built. She is second in size only to her sister ship, the *RMS Queen Elizabeth*. Permanently docked in the Long Beach Harbor, she will become a hotel and the only surviving ocean liner from the heyday of traveling the high seas in luxury and style.

## Spruce Goose
### Long Beach Harbor, 1947

November 2—Howard Hughes flies his Spruce Goose just one mile, the first and last flight of the biggest airplane ever built. The tail is almost eight stories high, and the wingspan wider than three football fields. The plane was built to transport troops and supplies to Europe during World War II, but by the time it was finished, the war was over. The Spruce Goose remains hidden from the public and shrouded in secrecy in a giant hangar in Long Beach Harbor until after Hughes's death in April 1976. In 1980 it goes on display in an enormous dome next to the *Queen Mary*. In 1990 it moves to the Evergreen International Aviation Museum in McMinnville, Oregon.

# Los Angeles County Fair Monorail
## Pomona, 1962

During the space age, monorails are predicted to revolutionize the future of transportation. Popular attractions at theme parks and world's fairs, they are high-class by any county fair standards. Fourteen monorail cars that look like travel trailers on pontoons were custom-designed for the fair and made in nearby Downey. In 1962, Richard Nixon cuts the ribbon and takes the first official ride on opening day. The monorail has a persistent problem in its first year: Pomona is very hot in September, and the monorail has no air conditioning. Worse yet, the giant windows don't open. So riders roast as they take in the mile-long bird's eye view of the fair. Despite the high cost of maintenance and mechanical problems, the monorail remains in service at the fairgrounds until 1990.

# Disneyland-Alweg Monorail
## Disneyland, Anaheim, 1959

Richard Nixon is also the first official passenger on Tomorrowland's "Highway in the Sky" when it is dedicated in 1959. The technology is from the German company Alweg. In the days leading up to the ribbon cutting and "first ride" ceremony, every time the engineers ran the monorail around the track for a test run it caught fire. On dedication day, the press and crowds of spectators gathered to watch the vice president,

Mrs. Nixon and their two lovely daughters (accompanied by a very nervous Walt Disney) as they boarded the futuristic transportation system on its first official voyage. They made it safely and nobody told Nixon that it was the first time the monorail completed a trip without catching fire.

# Autopia
## Disneyland, Anaheim, 1956

Cigarette, pinkie ring, Levis, turned-up collar and the perfect 1950s hair-do. This guy is waiting in line for the most popular original attraction in Tomorrowland, "The Freeway of the Future." Millions of children will drive a gasoline-powered car here for the very first time.

On Disneyland's opening day in 1955, Disney engineers didn't anticipate that people would want to treat these delicate fiberglass-bodied "European sports cars" as bumper cars. So just a couple of weeks after the park opened, the entire Autopia fleet was damaged or destroyed. The cars had to be repaired and fitted with wraparound bumpers to cushion the never-ending rear-end collisions. A new fleet of cars with an updated late-1950s design replaces the original vehicles in 1958. Autopia survives as the last standing original attraction in Tomorrowland.

# Park La Brea from the Goodyear Blimp
## Los Angeles, 1966

Unique by Southern California housing standards, the utopian towers and townhouses of Park La Brea seem very European in their lush park setting. The largest apartment community west of the Mississippi, the two-story townhomes were built in 1944, then followed by the towers in 1952. And it is pricey: tower units start at $105 a month. Built by the Metropolitan Life Insurance Company of New York, the housing community is named for Southern California's most historic curiosity, the redundantly named La Brea Tar Pits across the street.

# Freeway Interchange
## East Los Angeles, 1966

The vast expansion of the "toll-free"-way system in the 1950s and 1960s has made Southern California the most advanced metropolis on earth. More than anything else in the built environment, freeways define the modern era and forever change the landscape, lifestyle and distance between the city and suburbia. In 1940 the Arroyo Seco Parkway connecting downtown and Pasadena was L.A.'s first freeway. The network rapidly expanded into hundreds of miles of high-speed roadways that cross and merge on different levels without stoplights, revolutionizing transportation forever.

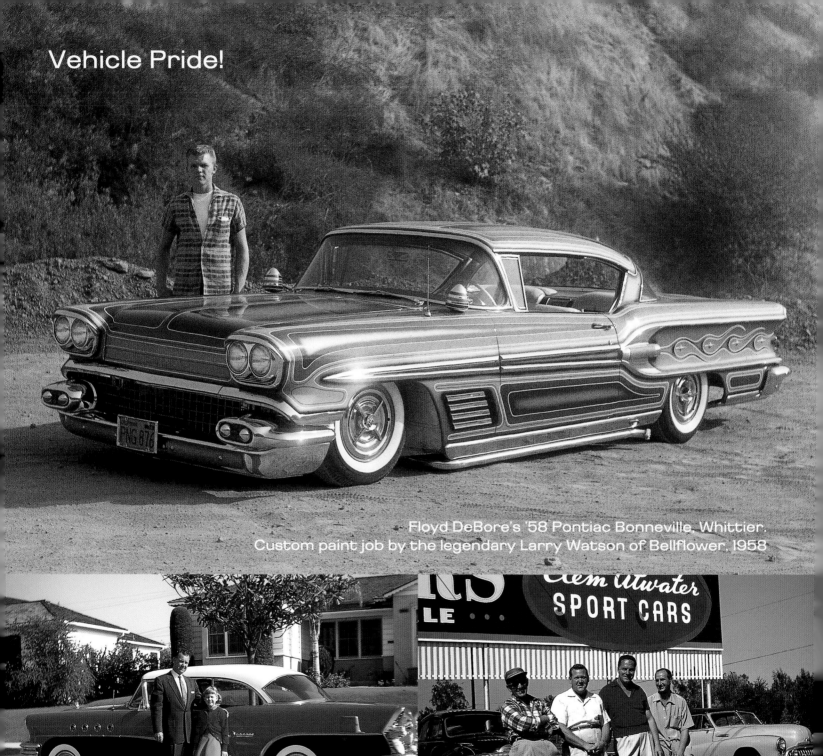

# Vehicle Pride!

Floyd DeBore's '58 Pontiac Bonneville, Whittier.
Custom paint job by the legendary Larry Watson of Bellflower, 1958

'55 Buick Century, Downey, 1959

Car Salesmen, Encino, 1956

The Browns, '53 Cadillac Coupe de Ville, Tarzana, 1957

'67 Oldsmobile Cutlass at the car wash, 1968

'58 Renault, Los Angeles, 1959

Jack and his '52 Ford delivery truck, Whittier, 1952

California Highway Patrol car: '58 Chevrolet Del Rey, 1958

Betty and her '56 Mercury Montclair, Whittier, 1958

# Frank & Helen DeGroat
## Huntington Park, 1956

Home sweet home is on Newell St. Frank & Helen DeGroat obsessively document their lives on film. Helen works at the phone company. She drives a '48 Plymouth, makes her own soap, chops wood and poses with exotic hibiscus flowers in front of the shower curtain. Frank is a police officer with the Huntington Park Police Department and a part-time employee at Shellman Plastics in South Gate.

# Dinner with the Kelloggs
## Alhambra, 1955

Ruffled curtains and California pottery. Lee Kellogg
obviously is proud of his wife Katie's cooking. On the
menu are meatloaf sandwiches on Van de Kamp's bread
with catsup, potato chips, cottage cheese and crushed
pineapple, olives and pickles. And by Katie's elbow,
an artichoke and a big stick of butter.

# Dessert with the DeGroats
## Huntington Park, 1955

More ruffled curtains, a cupboard full of Vernon California pottery and as many people as they can cram into their tiny breakfast nook. For dessert, Helen has made her sour cream cheesecake pie with its buttery, golden brown graham cracker crust and fresh strawberries on top. It's Frank birthday. He's taking the picture.

## Car Crash
### Corner of Packard and
### Orange Grove, Los Angeles, 1956

After a peaceful morning boating with friends on the lake at MacArthur Park near downtown Los Angeles, Gary Jacobson and his girlfriend Jackie, happen upon this car accident on their way home. He has his camera with him, loaded with film.

A 1953 Dodge Royal and a 1955 Buick Special have collided. The Dodge flipped on its side. A woman observes the scene standing with her hands on her hips, a man looks inside the car and two macho men pass by and don't seem to notice a thing. The police and the ambulance arrive. The Buick has a damaged hood, dented fender and turned-up "Dagmar" bumper tip, but the driver walks away. The Dodge driver is questioned by a flock of neighborhood ladies. What a miracle that no one is hurt!

# Time Trials
# at the Lions Drag Strip
## Long Beach, 1958

An MG, Porsche and Corvette pull up to the starting line. The timekeeper records their speed inside the tower. Beside the tower, a 1951 Pontiac ambulance and driver stand by. Spectators watch the excitement from behind the fence. Time trials allow drivers to test their speed, then tune their cars and try again for a faster time on the next run.

Anybody can race a car at Lions. Before it is permitted to run, each car is put into a class: sports car, modified or stock. Sports cars are the rarest entries. Modified cars are souped-up and require the most safety equipment. Stock cars are cars right off the street. Many teenagers "borrow" their parents' cars just to see how fast they can go at the drag strip. The only safety requirement for stock cars is that the hubcaps be removed so they won't fly off when the car reaches abnormally high speeds. Nobody wears seatbelts.

Local civic organizations in Pomona, Long Beach, Santa Ana and the San Fernando Valley create official drag strips to provide a safe alternative to racing on city streets and to promote cooperation between hot rodders and the police.

The Lions Drag Strip opened in 1955 and closes in 1972.

# Sunday Afternoon at the Races
## Culver City Speedway, 1953

The Weaver Brothers of San Fernando pose with their 1937 Pontiac, #33. They're out of the race. The grandstand is full of spectators who each paid a $1.25 to spend the afternoon watching cars race, roll and crash around a dusty dirt track. This is entry-level racing for anyone who wants to get into the sport. The cars are pre-war coupes, souped up with faster engines and fitted with seats and gas tanks left over from World War II airplanes. For safety, the bumpers and glass are removed and roll bars are installed. The fenders are trimmed to accommodate racing tires and the cars get bright new paint jobs. A series of elimination races qualifies the fastest cars for the main event, the last race of the day. Thirty laps. The big winner goes home with a tall trophy and a hundred bucks. Located just blocks from MGM Studios, Culver City Speedway opened in 1947 and closes in 1954.

# Compton Drive-In • Compton, 1977

By the 1970s Southern California has more outdoor screens than anywhere else in the world. The drive-in is the perfect combination of the region's two most influential elements, movies and cars. An enormous framed mural of Viking ships sailing on a choppy sea is labeled generously with the name of the city. This is by far the grandest and most artistic building in town. Built in 1949 by the largest local drive-in chain, Pacific Drive-In Theatres, it remains in business until its demolition in the 1990s.

The first-ever drive-in theater opened in New Jersey in 1934, the second, a year later at Pico and Westwood in Los Angeles.

# Sunset Drive-In Movie Theater
## Los Angeles County Fair, Pomona, 1952

The drive-in theater wasn't invented in Southern California but it was perfected here. This is the perfect miniature drive-in theater, appropriately named the Sunset. A television set doubles as a movie screen and shows the "feature" every night at dusk. It's one of the most charming features of the world's oldest and largest miniature garden railroad, a fixture at the L.A. County Fair since 1924. The cars in the parking lot are promotional toy models given to little boys while their parents shop for cars.

# Big Do-Nut DriveIn
## Los Angeles, 1951

The original twenty-two-foot stucco Big Do-Nut at the corner of Century and Normandie dwarfs a 1947 Cadillac. Grand opening night was July 10, 1950. One dozen donuts cost fifty-five cents. The biggest doughnut in the world is the genius idea of Russ Wendell, who worked as an automatic doughnut maker salesman. The gigantic doughnut is a magnet for customers who, for the first time ever, can buy doughnuts without getting out of their cars. Over the next six years, Wendell opens ten more stores in the Los Angeles area. In 1956, he will sell off his doughnut empire and begin another selling hot dogs and tacos at a chain of fast food stands called Pup 'n' Taco. The Big Do-Nut DriveIn will survive into the 21st century and its more famous sister store, Randy's Donuts near LAX, will become a symbol of Los Angeles.

# The Hot Dog Show
## Ontario, 1950

The name Hot Dog Show suggests a theater. But those stripes don't look like curtains, they look like a rather large person wearing red-and-white tights squatting, making those neon-trimmed hot dogs with angel wings and halos look not very appetizing. According to the owner Norma Jones, Joan Crawford pulled up in a big black limousine on her way to Palm Springs. Before ordering a round of hot dogs for her chauffeur, nanny and children, she insisted upon inspecting the cleanliness of the kitchen and bathroom. While the others sat on the patio and ate their hot dogs, Joan sat in the kitchen and smoked a cigarette. In 1960, the Hot Dog Show burns to the ground—grease fire in the kitchen.

# Jack in the Box at Dusk • Alhambra, 1964

An old-fashioned child's toy inspired the name, style and odd clown mascot of this "insured quality hamburger" chain whose original stand opened in San Diego in 1951. The "box" buildings were designed in 1958 in response to a local ordinance that limited the height of signs. The clever solution was to put four signboards together and form a box which had far more visual impact than the original sign. The International-Style-meets-fast-food design, decorated with color blocks and fake flying flags, looks like it was designed by Andy Warhol and Charles and Ray Eames. But no, it's simply fast food architecture at its best. Many of these vintage Jack in the Box buildings are updated in the 1970s by disguising them with a mansard roof.

# McDonald's in the Afternoon • Alhambra, 1954

This is the fifth McDonald's store built. By the time it opened in 1953, the McDonald brothers had already sold over nine million burgers. The enterprising brothers started with a traditional drive-in restaurant in San Bernardino in 1940. In 1948 they came up with an idea to streamline their operation by eliminating the carhops and everything on the menu that required a knife, fork and plate. That left them with hamburgers and French fries served from walk-up windows. Consider it the birth of the fast food business. Before they franchised in

1952, they hired architect Stanley Meston of Fontana to design a building that people would notice a block away. With Speedee as a mascot and the voluptuous Golden Arches, the result was stylish. Its angular roof, red-and-white striped tile and slanted windows showcase the innovative operation inside. Speedee will remain until 1964 and the shapely hamburger stands are built until 1968. The McDonald's at the corner of Lakewood and Florence in Downey will be the last of the original buildings to survive.

# White Front
## Anaheim, 1961

Giant, bright color blocks and a grand
space-age style awning entrance studded
with recessed spotlights glorify White
Front, one of Southern California's first
"big box" discount chain stores. Inside there
is no mood lighting like you find in department stores—just a dropped ceiling full of
bright fluorescent lights. The parking lot is
full. On the left is a brand new top-of-the-
line 1961 Ford Country Squire station wagon
finished in mint green and fake wood trim.
A 1959 Chevrolet with gull-wing tail fins and
cat's-eye taillights is parked on the right.
White Front first opened with a small store
in Watts in 1955. The owner was a man by
the name of Mr. Blackman who drove a
white Cadillac. Why is this store called
White Front when it's so colorful?

# Covina Bowl
## Covina, 1956

Vintage slides of bowling alleys are very rare. This one is particularly special because it shows Southern California's first ultra-modern deluxe bowling center just months after it opened in 1955. Inside there are thirty lanes, a billiard room, coffee shop, banquet rooms, beauty salon and nursery where a registered nurse babysits kids while mothers bowl in housewife leagues. The Pyramid Room cocktail lounge hosts musical acts such as the Ink Spots and risqué comedienne Rusty Warren, who will record a live album here. The Bowl is fashionably decorated in a coral-and-turquoise color scheme with Egyptian murals and hieroglyphics.

Archaeologists have found ancient cave drawings of people playing a game that looks like bowling. After ages of evolution, the game finally got the respect it deserved in the late 1940s after AMF invented a machine that changed the game forever, the automatic pin spotter. This modern invention eliminated the need for young delinquents and drunken old men who usually reset the pins and contributed to the game's low-class reputation. In the late 1950s, the image of bowling has skyrocketed and it's suburbia's favorite sport. Deluxe bowling centers are more than bowling alleys—they're twenty-four-hour social, sport and entertainment centers.

Covina Bowl is one of few '50s bowling alleys to survive into the twenty-first century.

# Eastland Shopping Center
## West Covina, 1957

An Erector Set-style stained-glass sign tower! If that doesn't catch your eye as you speed by at sixty miles per hour on the new stretch of the San Bernardino Freeway, the May Company's huge "M" will. Eastland just had its grand opening and it's the first freeway-side shopping center in Southern California. A spectacular International Style retail island, Eastland is surrounded by an ocean of asphalt luxuriously divided into thousands of parking spaces. The future of retail has arrived.

Up the outdoor escalators, modern specialty stores line a promenade with splashy fountains, modern garden art and piped-in Muzak, to complete the out-of-this-world environment. At Clifton's Cafeteria, an offspring of the original in downtown Los Angeles, an organist serenades diners. No unsightly loading docks are visible to shoppers; to keep delivery trucks out of sight, a half-mile-long tunnel connects the basements of the stores. In the event of a nuclear attack—no problem! The tunnel doubles as a designated Civil Defense Fallout Shelter equipped to house thousands of civilians for up to a week.

This utopian marketplace and the many others that it will inspire are welcome alternatives to the old-fashioned, congested Main Street shopping districts throughout Southern California.

# Alpha Beta • Arcadia, 1960

Crisco is Alpha Beta's most prominently displayed product. It is the week of June 20 according to the cover of *Time Magazine*.

     A long-time Southern California grocery store chain, Alpha Beta began in Pasadena as the Triangle Grocerteria. The name change came in 1928 when the owners began organizing the shelves with products in alphabetical order. "Alpha Beta" began as a merchan-

dising concept, not as a store name, and was first used at the Pomona store in 1917. In 1963, the supermarket chain will expand into the restaurant business and spin off a chain of coffee shops called Alphy's. The last Alpha Beta will close in the mid-1990s, a casualty of a supermarket merger.

# Thriftimart • Los Angeles, 1962

Thriftimart is spelled out in an optimistic handwritten font, and a big "T" stakes its claim. This is no grocery store—this a supermarket! Sci-fi flying saucer fixtures line a promenade leading to doors that open automatically. The inside is air conditioned and there is plenty of parking.

Supermarket grand openings have become big events. There are always searchlights attracting attention from miles around, and often kiddy rides, clowns, live music and an occasional appearance by the Oscar Meyer Wienermobile. Contest give-aways are the main attraction. Crowds sign up for a chance to win everything from a free bag of groceries, to an electric fryer, to a beautiful brand new car proudly displayed by a local automobile dealership.

# Fire!
## Sunland, 1955

A blazing brush fire sweeps over the hill. A family is caught in the act of panic and heroism. Mom runs across the yard of her tudor-ranch style tract home in the foothills. A striped T-shirted and suspendered little boy takes in the startling scene from the sidewalk. In front of him, a soap-box derby car is in mid-construction. In the driveway, a brand-new 1955 two-tone Dodge Royal Sierra station wagon. Up on the roof, two boys battle to save the house with a garden hose. The dog just stands there. The La Tuna Canyon Fire, caused by a tipped-over backyard BBQ, will burn for five days.

## Groundbreaking Photo Op
### Torrance, 1953

Tract home developers pose proudly on an old horse-drawn wagon left over from the pioneer days as they celebrate what they are about to do: transform acres of former farmland into a perfect suburban neighborhood. The colorful billboard advertises more than just the three-bedroom, two-bath homes. "Year 'Round Recreation" and the Southern California lifestyle are what's for sale.

# Tract Homes for Sale on Easy Street
## Highland Park, 1958

At the corner of Easy Street and Fortune Way a fluorescent orange sign points buyers to the sales office. In this tract, buyers have their choice of at least two different styles, the more subdued rock-roof model trimmed with rectangles or the more exotic Pagoda ranch with an enormous Asian symbol on the garage door.

Southern California is the tract home capital of the world. The homes are designed to be built on a mass scale at low cost. Many are sold before they are even completed. The great demand requires quick construction.

# The Perfect Model Tract Home
## Monterey Park, 1958

This is more than the perfect tract home—it's a dream house. Enormous sliding glass doors, modern furniture on high heels flanking the fireplace, lamps with drum shades and wall-to-wall carpet—could a suburban couple ask for more? An adjustable UFO light fixture hovers above the Danish Modern dining room set. A rubber tree plant and a split-leaf philodendron add a little oxygen to an otherwise synthetic interior. The final touch to show some class: a hand-carved African figurine from an exotic import shop.

# The Perfect Suburban Couple
## Monterey Park, 1960

They bought the model home! It's six o'clock in the
evening. Mood music is playing on the stereo console
and Mr. Suburbia has just returned home from a day
at the office. If they want to enjoy a cigarette before
dinner, no problem—they can smoke right, they can
smoke left or they can smoke forward. Mrs. Suburbia's
free-form, swimming pool-shaped ashtray is full.
Looks like she's been smoking all day.

# Poolside
## Encino, 1962

Hello! A Coppertone tan, striped bongo drums, the most stylish piece of patio furniture ever made and a telephone with an extra-long cord, all next to a big sparkling swimming pool. This young man is living the American dream, laying out by the pool in sunny Southern California.

## Poolside
### Azusa, 1959

Cigarettes, booze, sunglasses, a tam o'shanter topped with a yellow yarn poof ball, terrycloth robe and slippers. This man is trying to be glamorous by the pool doing the Hollywood movie director look . . . but in Azusa?

# Swingin' Pool and Patio Party at Nellie & Palmer Bailey's
## Los Angeles, 1957

A shapely swimming pool, candlelight, empty cocktail glasses, abalone ashtrays, exotic Japanese-style pillow seating and a round Formica-topped lounge—what a party! At left in the center back and climbing out of the pool are the host and hostess, Nellie & Palmer Bailey.

She owns a bar at the Farmers Market at 3rd and Fairfax called The Chatterbox, and he is an insurance salesman. They have no children and their parties are strictly adults only. Their guests are regulars who seem to get along very well.

# Backyard BBQ • Arcadia, 1960

Father-and-son portrait with truck, "catch of the day," and backyard barbecue. The 1957 Chevrolet truck is striking in Matador Red. According to what is written on the slide mount, the catch of the day is "Trout caught in the San Gabriel River."

Cooking outdoors over an open flame has been around since the beginning of mankind, so it's no surprise that the barbecue brings out the caveman in every suburban dad. The portable backyard barbecue didn't come of age until the 1950s. By 1960 no suburban household is complete without one.

# Associated Executives Club Backyard Masquerade Party
## Arcadia, 1959

Dinner is served on the patio: roast suckling pig on a bed of coconut with mandarin orange slices. On the spine, sliced pineapple with maraschino cherry centers. Around the neck, a double string of black and green olives. And so the pig can see who's eating him, an olive slice eyeball with a pimento pupil. In its mouth, the traditional apple. Since this is Southern California, it only makes sense that there's a lemon too. After dinner, the party guests, couple by couple, pose for the photographer to show off their clever costumes, pictured on the next page.

Associated Executives Club
Backyard Masquerade Party
Arcadia, 1959

# Farmer John
## Vernon, 1962

These block-long, hand-painted murals on the exterior walls of the Farmer John meat-packing plant are the grandest and most charming works of art in town. Deep in the heart of hardcore industrial Los Angeles, the quaint tromp l'oeil pig farm scenes look like they came out of a children's storybook, yet they mask the horrors of what goes on inside the facility. Farmer John is the largest pork slaughterhouse on the West Coast.

Homespun and family-run, Farmer John started on 1931. In 1953, Hollywood scenic painter Les Grimes began to paint the delightful murals. He will continue to expand, enhance and maintain the murals until 1968, when he tragically loses his footing, falls from the scaffolding and dies. His murals survive attacks by vandals and vegetarians, and become a local landmark.

# Mineral Baths
## Desert Hot Springs, 1954

This is Mr. Walker of Monrovia. And yes, he has man-breasts. If Mr. Walker wants to lay out in the hot desert sun, he can—there's a foot or so between the wall and the pool. If he wants to get comfortable in a chaise lounge, there aren't any; a park bench will have to do. If he needs a lifeguard, too bad, he's gone! And by the way, there is no parking by the pool—the curb is red.

Hundreds of thousands of acres of beautiful undis-
turbed desert scenery and someone had to build a wall
around this place and paint in the scenery. It should be
called the Painted Desert Inn.

# Ike & Mamie Arrive
## Palm Springs, 1962

Former President Dwight D. Eisenhower and his First Lady Mamie have just pulled up in their big black 1960 Imperial Crown. It's nearly twenty-feet long, weighs almost three tons, costs $16,000 and is the most powerful and best-handling formal car on the road. A thin chrome bead highlights the wheel wells, bumper and soaring tail fins. The taillights have "floating" chrome Saturn rings around them. This one was specially built for the President, who lived in the White

House from 1953 through 1962. The chauffeur holds the
door open as they step out into the dirt. A man leans
in to shake Mamie's gloved hand.

Moments later, when Ike blows his nose and the
First Lady giggles, two little boys curiously peek inside
the car. The whole time there are people peeking
through the bushes. Where's the Secret Service?

# Leisure World
## Seal Beach, 1962

This giant globe set in a fountain marks the entrance to Leisure World. In 1964 the world-famous Unisphere, a giant globe that's also set in a fountain, will become the logo and centerpiece of the New York World's Fair. The globes bear a remarkable resemblance. But the Leisure World globe spins and the Unisphere doesn't.

Retirement communities came of age this year, as Leisure World and Sun City opened within a month of each other in 1962. Leisure World is promoted as "the best world of all," Its first residents moved in on June 6.

# Harry's Sister and Her Husband
## Sun City, 1966

A giant spotlit tiki god is set off-center in a grass circle near the entrance to Sun City's own Greek Theatre. He is perfect for the over-sixty-five set to pose with and idolize. Located just northeast of Indio, Sun City was built by prolific developer Del Webb and promoted as an "active retirement community." The advertising slogan is "We are selling not just a house, but a way of life." After the grand opening on June 15, 1962, the fourteen thousand acres of homes, shops, clubhouses, golf courses and tiki gods were an instant success. The simple little homes ranged from $11,950 to $17,950. An additional $1,900 got you a house on a fairway.

# Pan-Pacific Auditorium
## Los Angeles, 1953

Four Streamline Moderne flagpole towers mark the entrance to Southern California's premier indoor special events center, built in 1935. Ice shows, roller skating competitions, home shows, custom car shows, rodeos, sporting events and political rallies attract huge crowds. In 1957, Elvis Presley rocks the house of nine thousand fans wearing his famous gold lamé suit. By the late 1960s, after the Los Angeles Convention Center is built downtown, the Pan Pacific falls out of favor, and worse, into disrepair. In the early 1980s, the auditorium is demolished, but the legendary flagpole towers are saved and slated for restoration. But in 1989, just weeks before the work is to begin, the famous façade of this architectural icon catches fire and is completely destroyed.

## Brown Derby
### Los Angeles, 1948

A giant hat became the most famous restaurant in the world. The first of four Brown Derby restaurants, and the only one shaped like the namesake hat, the original at the corner of Wilshire Boulevard and Alexandria was built in 1926. The location couldn't have been more ideal, right across the street from the most fashionable hotel in town, the Ambassador, and the world-famous night club, the Coconut Grove. But by the mid-1960s, the novelty wears off and the glamour fades. The legendary restaurant is no longer a place to see and be seen. In 1979, developers buy the property and announce plans to demolish the aging landmark and to build a mini-mall in its place. Preservationists vociferously oppose that plan, so the developers compromise and build the mini-mall with the legendary hat on the roof.

# The Hub of Hollywood
## Vine Street, Hollywood, 1948

Rooftop neon signs, Streamline Moderne architecture, taxicabs, bowling, dancing, shopping, restaurants, coffee shops, offices, recording and radio studios—this is the hub of Hollywood. This is Vine Street looking north from Sunset Boulevard towards Hollywood Boulevard. It's the heyday of radio, just before television changes everything.

Tom Breneman's national radio variety show on ABC, *Breakfast in Hollywood*, broadcasts live every weekday morning from his Polynesian-themed restaurant. Breneman's stylish white Streamline building becomes ABC radio studios in 1949. CBS operates a studio up the street behind the red billboard. NBC Radio City in Hollywood is here, at the corner of Sunset and Vine.

In the 1970s, the Streamline Moderne building becomes the home of the *Merv Griffin Show*. After many years of decline, the building gets restored and becomes the historic centerpiece of a block-long housing and retail development.

# NBC Radio City
## Hollywood, 1948

Monumental Moderne at the northeast corner of Sunset and Vine. Built in 1934, NBC is the most famous radio studio in Hollywood, home to Red Skelton, Fanny Brice, Bob Hope and many other legendary radio stars who performed their shows here in front of studio audiences. In 1955 NBC builds "Color City" in Burbank, with state-of-the-art television studios. In 1964, this landmark Hollywood building is considered an unimportant relic from "the old days" of radio and is demolished to make room for a Home Savings Bank building.

# Our First Television
## El Monte, 1950

Dark forest green walls, a fan in the window, a slot machine, a patio chair and the family's first television, a $189.95 1949 Motorola. This is an early home entertainment center. Did the manual that came with that TV say to paint the room the darkest color that you can find and put a fan in the window to blow cool air on those hot TV tubes? And don't bother with a comfortable piece of furniture—bring something in from the patio.

The little boy isn't interested in the television. All he wants to do is go flying at Streamland Park.

# Streamland Park • Pico Rivera, 1950

Named for the stream that runs through it, this fifty-acre outdoor recreation facility began as a picnic ground in 1930. Before long, it had expanded to include a baseball diamond, bandstand, dance floor, picnic tables, barbeque pits and miniature golf course. The kiddy park is the perfect example of pre-Disneyland rides that just go 'round and 'round.

      The main attraction is the Venice Miniature

Railroad. When Abbot Kinney developed Venice around 1900, he wanted a trolley to go between the boardwalk, beach and canals. He couldn't afford it, so he settled for this miniature steam train which ran from 1905 to 1925. In 1935 it was discovered in a scrap yard. In 1946 it was restored and found a new home at Streamland Park. In 1968 the park closes to make way for tract homes.

# Pony Cart Ice Cream & Pet Parade • San Pedro, 1947

An old-fashioned canvas-shaded cart complete with fringe stops in the middle of the 2700 block of cement-paved Denison Avenue. Two brothers have their picture taken on a pony while their playmates hop aboard the cart and choose a frozen treat. An enterprising street vendor offers the unlikely combination of ice cream, Popsicles and "Free Pony Rides at Your Birthday Party." The cart is equipped with a speaker amplifying canned carnival music and has fluorescent night lights for the horses and refrigerated bins.

Those same Pony Cart Ice Cream ponies appear in the pet parade at the corner of Twelfth and Gaffey. Neighbors gather as the kids pass by with their baby buggies trimmed in bright crepe paper, red wagons and special parade vehicles for the dog, cat, horse and pony promenade, all sponsored by a local civic group.

# Luer "Quality Meat" Rocket
## Sunland, 1955

This flatbed-bound rocket came to life from the pages of Frankie Luer's Space Adventures, a comic book published by Luer, a local meat packing house that started in downtown Los Angeles in 1885. What the Wienermobile is to Oscar Meyer, this rocket is to Luer. It tours Southern California, making appearances in local parades, supermarket grand openings and other civic events promoting "quality meat" products. Costumed spokesmodels are aboard for the ride. The middle model poses in a Roy Rogers/ Buck Rogers look— cowboy boots with her spacesuit. In 1997 the Luer Rocket is discovered in a Prescott, Arizona junkyard, in weathered but restorable condition.

# Captain Jet, 4th of July Parade
## Sunland, 1955

Adoring young fans and one big bruiser in a leather
jacket and cuffed Levi's rush KNXT-TV Channel 2 star,
Captain Jet, for an autograph as he waves from a
1952 Oldsmobile Ninety-Eight. Captain Jet introduces
cartoons and other children's entertainment on a
local weekday-morning program. It was the first
Los Angeles-based kids' show to air reruns of *The Little
Rascals* and *Laurel & Hardy* comedies.

# Hot Dogs and Beauty Queens, Date Festival
## Indio, 1966

Queen Sheherezade and her court of princesses parade in a 1965 Ford Galaxie past a Hot Dog on a Stick stand. Hot Dog on a Stick started at Muscle Beach in Santa Monica in 1946 selling corn dogs "made with grandma's recipe." The Date Festival started in Indio in 1921 to promote and celebrate Coachella Valley's annual date harvest. In 1947, the Arabian Nights theme was adopted in honor of the date's Middle Eastern origins. The Riverside County Fair and the Date Festival takes place every February. In 2002, after fifty-five years, the fair's Middle Eastern theme is dropped due to negative world politics.

# The Hood Ornament Pose
## Muscle Beach, Santa Monica, 1957

Is this man feeling cool ocean breezes in places where we don't ordinarily feel cool ocean breezes? America's obsession with fitness began in the 1930s on Santa Monica's sunny shores. In the beginning, Muscle Beach was as much about breathtaking acrobatics as it was about strength and muscles. Young men and women wearing revealing swimwear did somersaults, handstands and built human pyramids. Hollywood talent scouts were often among the crowds of onlookers seeking beefcake and cheesecake to cast in movies and television.

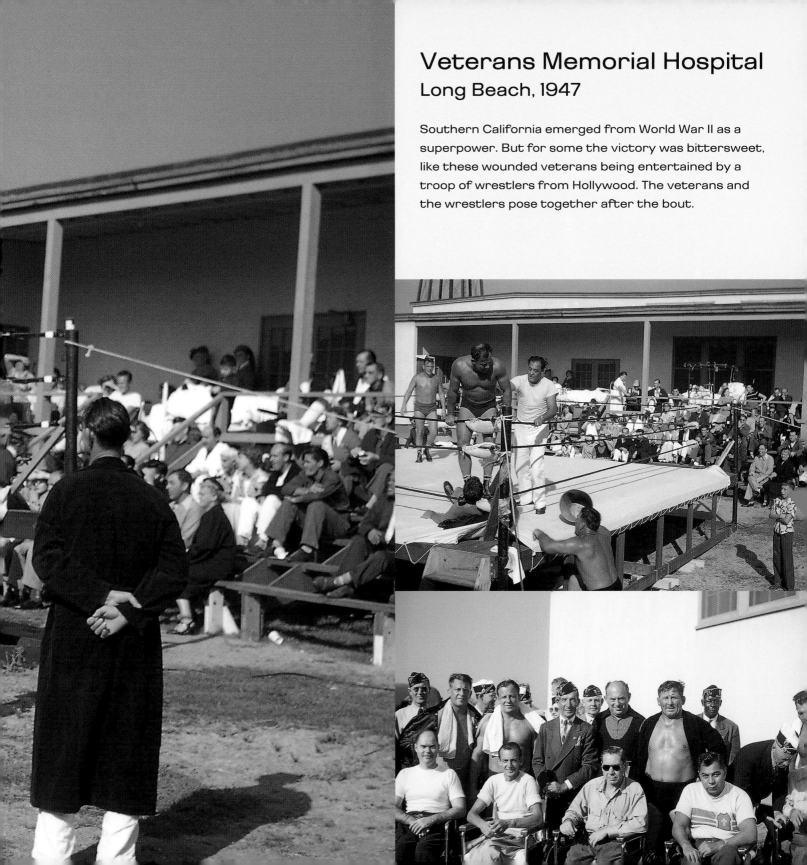

# Veterans Memorial Hospital
## Long Beach, 1947

Southern California emerged from World War II as a superpower. But for some the victory was bittersweet, like these wounded veterans being entertained by a troop of wrestlers from Hollywood. The veterans and the wrestlers pose together after the bout.

# Easter Sunday
# at the
# Desert Inn
## Palm Springs, 1953

Waiters and waitresses, a giant cut-out Easter bunny
and enormous building blocks. Privileged children of
the rich and famous celebrate Easter dressed in
their best.

# Christmas Morning at the Desert Inn
## Palm Springs, 1953

Palm trees, sunshine and Santa. The Desert Inn is the heart and soul of Palm Springs society, and is paving the way for the all of the fashionable desert resorts and motels that will eventually come to the desert. The Inn opened in 1915 as a sanitarium where sick people could convalesce in the warm, dry atmosphere . But in 1926, the name was changed to the Desert Inn and the brochure stated: "no invalids or people with communicable diseases." In 1967 the Inn will be demolished to make room for the Desert Fashion Plaza mall.

## Christmas Eve Family Portrait
### Downey, 1964

Mr. & Mrs. Norman Miller and their daughter Iona, modeling her Christmas cowgirl suit, pose ankle-deep in fake snow. Behind them is their signature big fake snowman. A pink Prancer cut-out is prancing in front of them. He matches the house, has long eyelashes and sparkles with glitter.

# Christmas Morning
## Downey, 1965

Flirtatious with parted red lips, winking long lashes, and welcoming handless arms, this spotlit snowman creation has grown to enormous proportions and has become more of a snow monster.

Decorating the yard with yards and yards of cotton batting and tinfoil icicles hanging from the eaves for Christmas is an annual tradition for the Millers. It takes them days to create their very special winter wonderland. But they excel in more than holiday yard decor. They work together full-time selling Tupperware, and in 1968 become the top-selling husband-and-wife sales team in the Unites States. Their hobby is square dancing.

# Camellia Festival Floats
## Temple City, 1957

A cow, kangaroo and sailboat covered in camellias–only in Temple City. The pushcart floats are designed and decorated by local youth groups. In 1944, a Temple City women's group had a contest to choose the city flower and slogan. Their town became the "Home of Camellias." For the first Camellia Festival parade a year later, an eight-month-old baby girl was crowned queen. She rode in an open car down Las Tunas Drive as Camp Fire Girls handed out camellia blossoms.

In 1948, local children were invited to decorate their doll buggies and bicycles with camellias, then parade to the beat of the "Camellia Festival March," written by a local composer. The community showed up en masse. Within a few years every service and civic organization in town was involved. The event blossomed into a weekend festival that included the camellia parade, camellia carnival, camellia show and coronation of the camellia court composed of a king, queen, two princes and two princesses, who were always first graders. Festival organizers hoped that after being chosen as camellia royalty the children would want to join one of the city's youth organizations. The parade has become an annual tradition.

# Tournament of Roses Parade • Pasadena

A pampas-grass Jesus Christ chia pet is sponsored by the Lutheran Hour gospel radio program in 1953. In 1957, Alhambra's float teaches history, showing the evolution of the telephone. Surprisingly the Young Republicans get the 1955 Award of Merit for their lackluster "Integrity in Government" float. In 1954, the Shriners have a giant fez on their float. In 1957, Van Nuys gives us the ugliest float of all time—The Frost on the Pumpkin. But in 1958, Van Nuys comes back with the greatest

Rose Parade float of all time—Cherry Pie à la Mode.

The New Year's Day spectacle started in 1890 when members of Pasadena's high-society Valley Hunt Club celebrated the holiday by decorating their horses and buggies with flowers and parading down Colorado Boulevard. The parade became another opportunity to promote the region's mild winter climate and abundance of flowers to easterners and midwesterners.

# On the Set of
## *The Ten Commandments*
### Paramount Studios, Hollywood, 1956

Lights! Camera! Action! A blue screen, two teamsters, six lights, hundreds of extras, and three hundred thousand gallons of water. Charlton Heston as Moses is parting the Red Sea. It's the big scene in one of the biggest movies of all time. This is a rare behind-the-scenes shot taken on the set as the film was rolling. *The Ten Commandments* was a Biblical epic of the highest order complete with scenes shot on location in Egypt, spectacular colorful sets and costumes and literally a "cast of thousands." It was filmed in wide-screen Vista-Vision and saturated Technicolor. In 1957, it is the highest-grossing film and goes on to be one of the most successful movies of all time. Some consider it to be a cinematic masterpiece—many consider it one of their favorite movies.

The parting of the Red Sea is one of the most impressive pre-computer-generated special effects in the history of cinema. It was achieved by using the same technique director Cecil B. DeMille perfected in his 1923 version of *The Ten Commandments*. Two blocks of gelatin were placed side-by-side, melted with blow torches and shot in extreme close-up. The footage was then seen in reverse.

Sleeping Beauty's Castle, 1957

Fantasyland, 1963

Tomorrowland man, 1962

Disneyland
Anaheim

Main Street USA, 1956

Main Street, USA, 1960

Frontierland, 1957

Tom Sawyer's Island, 1958

House of the Future, 1965

# The New Tomorrowland
## Disneyland, Anaheim, 1968

Far in the distance through the palm trees, the Columbia Ship is sailing the Rivers of America in Frontierland—a startling contrast to the soaring rockets and futuristic mass-transit system of the new Tomorrowland. The original Tomorrowland was completely remodeled in 1967. The new Tomorrowland is an ultramodern out-of-this world environment, where even Monsanto's popular House of the Future is considered passé. Existing attractions have been made over or paved over and new ones have been added. The Astro-Jets have moved three flights up and are now the towering, spinning centerpiece—the Rocket Jets. The Circarama Theater is now the CircleVision Theater premiering *America the Beautiful*, a travelogue film projected in the round. Flight to the Moon is now called Rocket to the Moon. Monsanto has replaced its Hall of Chemistry with Adventure Thru Innerspace, where guests "shrink" and explore the world of molecules and atoms while listening to the theme song, "Miracles from Molecules." The all new Goodyear-sponsored PeopleMover is inspired by the Magic Skyway, a ride Disney designed for Ford Motor Company to present at the 1964 New York World's Fair. From a moving platform, passengers board the plastic cars that have tilt-up canopies for ease of entry. The PeopleMover takes them on a mile-long track through various attractions in Tomorrowland, including the star attraction, General Electric's Carousel of Progress.

## Carousel of Progress, Tomorrowland
### Disneyland, Anaheim, 1973

A charming computer-operated mannequin family speak and sing the pleasures and wonders of household progress and electricity. The four acts take place in the 1890s, 1920s, 1940s and the future. Each act plays to a different audience at the same time. When the act ends, guests remain in their seats and the whole theater revolves to the next fixed stage set for the next act. This image is the final act—Christmas sometime beyond 1973. Sheer curtains over floor-to-ceiling glass are drawn just enough to reveal the focal point, the perfect city in the perfect distance. Gifts are everywhere—among them, electric curlers, a toaster oven and hair dryer, all thanks to the sponsor, General Electric. Disney originally created this spectacular theatrical time machine for G.E. at the 1964 New York World's Fair. When the Fair ended it was transplanted in its entirety to the new Tomorrowland as the main attraction. Even though it closes in 1972, the Carousel of Progress is my all-time favorite attraction at Disneyland.

Date Grove Family Portrait
Indio, 1954

Southern Californialand : Mid-Century Culture in Kodachrome
Copyright © 2004 by Charles Phoenix, www.godblessamericana.com
Designed by Amy Inouye, www.futurestudio.com

First edition
10 9 8 7 6 5 4 3 2 1
ISBN 1-883318-42-4

Library of Congress Cataloging-in-Publication Data

Phoenix, Charles, 1962-
Southern Californialand : mid-century culture in Kodachrome / by Charles Phoenix.
p. cm.
ISBN 1-883318-42-4 (hardcover : alk. paper)
1. California, Southern--Social life and customs--20th century--Pictorial works. 2. Popular culture--California, Southern--History--20th century--Pictorial works. 3. California, Southern--History, Local--Pictorial works. 4. California, Southern--Social life and customs--20th century. 5. Popular culture--California, Southern--History--20th century. I. Title.
F867.P525 2004
979.4'053--dc22
2004001812

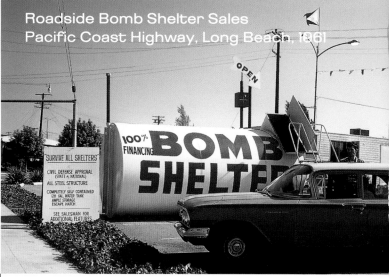

Roadside Bomb Shelter Sales
Pacific Coast Highway, Long Beach, 1961

Wigwam Village
Rialto, 1955

THANK YOU: Margaret Adamic, Tony Baxter, Rich Borowy, Charles Coverdale, Bruce Emerton, Charles Fish, Pat Ganahl, Jason Garcia, Dick and Eileen Garson, Bruce Gordon, Jackie Green, D-J Haanraadts, Karen Hillenberg, Nick Hironis, Gary Jacobson, Patrick Jenkins, Norma Jones, Darius Long, Tom Luce, Ben McGinty, Ed Leibowitz and Mary Melton, Chris Merritt, Chuck Morrell, Roz Music, Chris Nichols, Thom and Lisa Taylor, Michael Uhlenkott, Larry Underhill and Jim Walker.

SPECIAL THANKS: Paddy Calistro, Scott McAuley and Amy Inouye.

Printed in China

ANGEL CITY PRESS
2118 Wilshire Boulevard #880
Santa Monica, California 90403
310.395.9982
www.angelcitypress.com